PIANO . VOCAL . GUITAR

ROADHOUSE COUNTRY

ISBN 978-1-5400-0399-7

HAL•LEONARD®
7777 W. BLUEMOUND RD. P.O. BOX 13819 MILWAUKEE, WI 53213

Visit Hal Leonard Online at
www.halleonard.com

ACT NATURALLY

Words and Music by VONIE MORRISON
and JOHNNY RUSSELL

They're _____ gon-na put me in the mov - ies,
make the scene ___ a-bout a man that's sad and lone - ly, _____ and

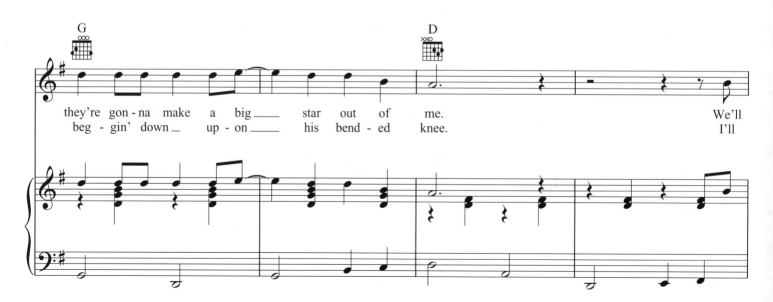

they're gon-na make a big____ star out of me.
beg-gin' down ___ up-on ___ his bend-ed knee.

We'll
I'll

make a film _ a - bout a man that's sad and lone - ly,   and
play the part, _   but I won't need re-hears - in';

all I got - ta do is   act nat - 'ral - ly.
all I have to do is   act nat - 'ral - ly.   Well, I

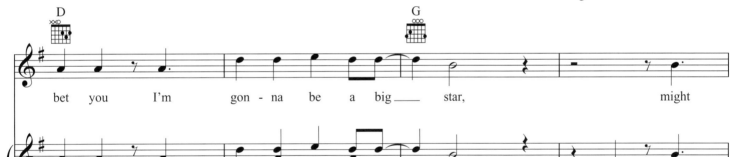

bet you I'm gon - na be a big _ star,   might

win an Os - car,   you can _ nev - er tell. _   The

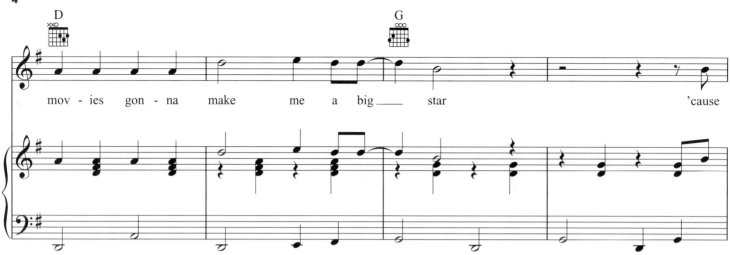

mov - ies gon - na make me a big___ star 'cause

I can play the part ___ so well. ___ Well, I

hope you come and see me in the mov - ies,

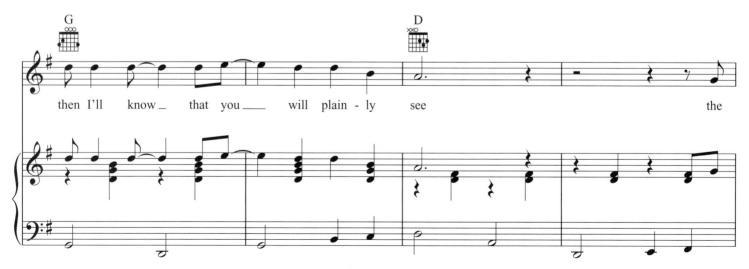

then I'll know_ that you___ will plain - ly see the

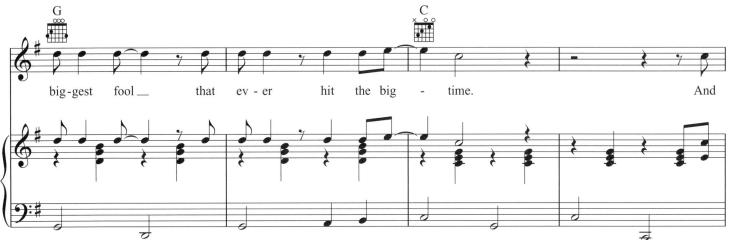

big-gest fool ___ that ev - er hit the big - time.   And

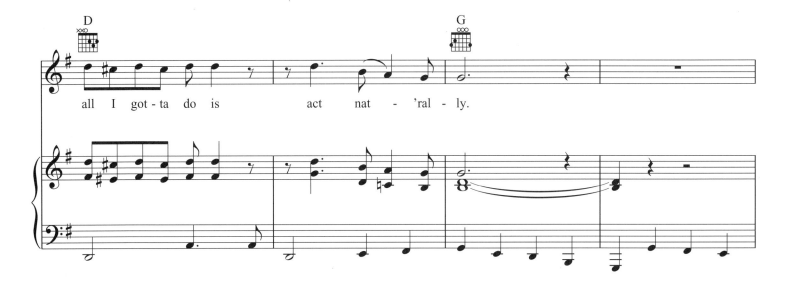

all I got - ta do is act nat - 'ral - ly.

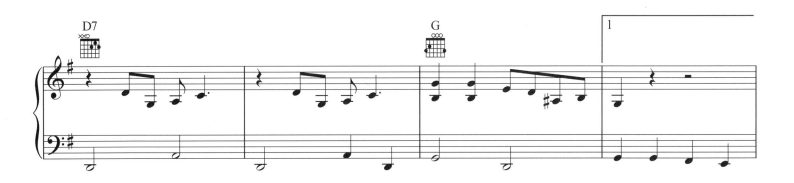

We'll

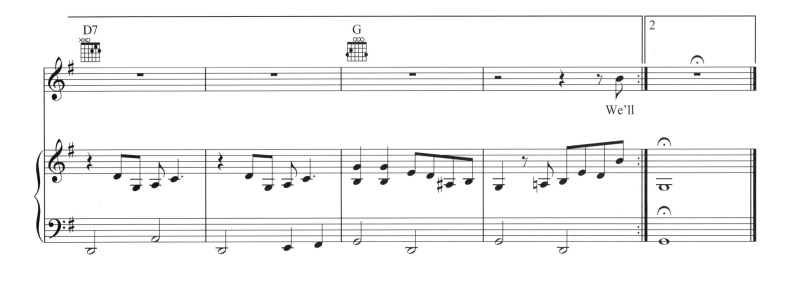

ALL MY EX'S LIVE IN TEXAS

Words and Music by LYNDIA J. SHAFER
and SANGER D. SHAFER

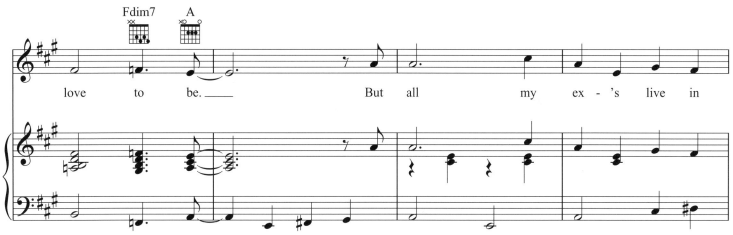

love to be. ____ But all my ex-'s live in

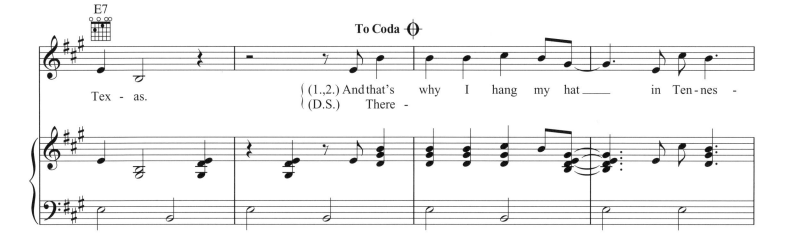

Tex - as.

(1.,2.) And that's why I hang my hat ____ in Ten - nes -
(D.S.) There -

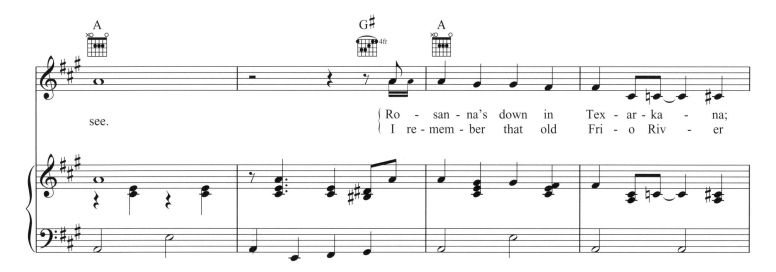

see.

Ro - san - na's down in Tex - ar - ka - na;
I re - mem - ber that old Fri - o Riv - er

want - ed me to push her broom. And sweet I - lene's in
where I learned to ____ swim. And it brings to mind an -

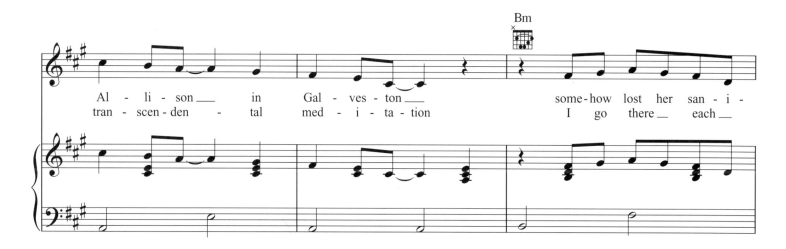

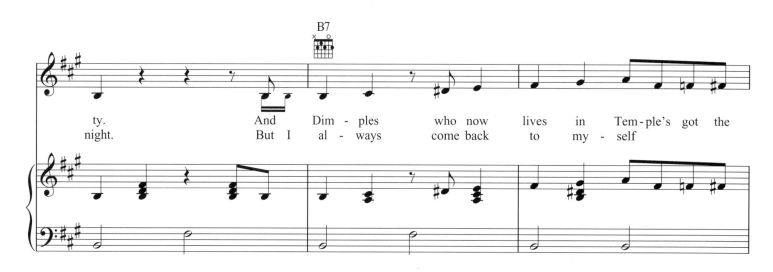

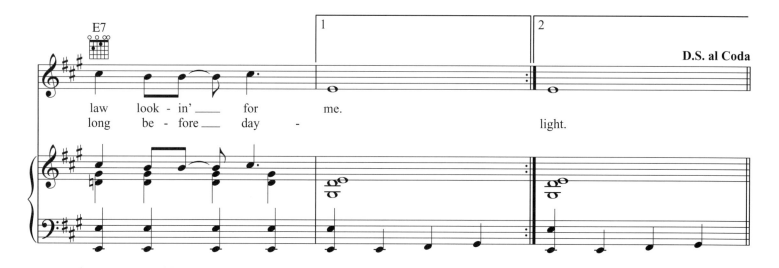

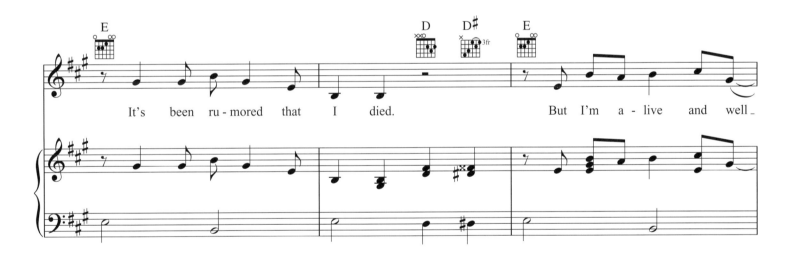

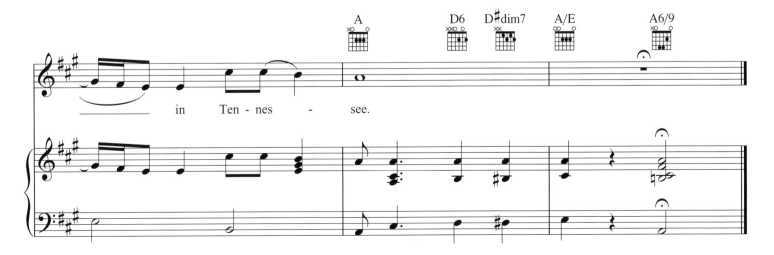

COAL MINER'S DAUGHTER

Words and Music by
LORETTA LYNN

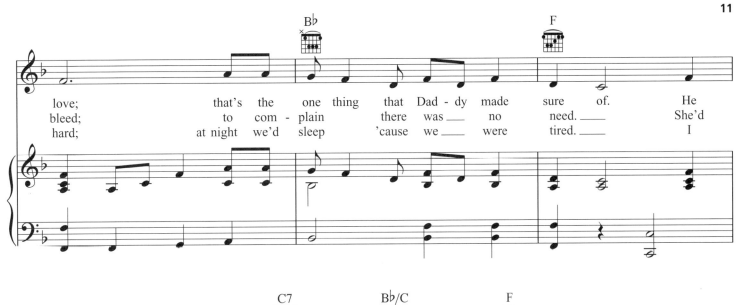

love; / bleed; / hard;
that's the one thing that Dad - dy made sure of. He / to com - plain there was __ no need. __ She'd / at night we'd sleep 'cause we __ were tired. __ I

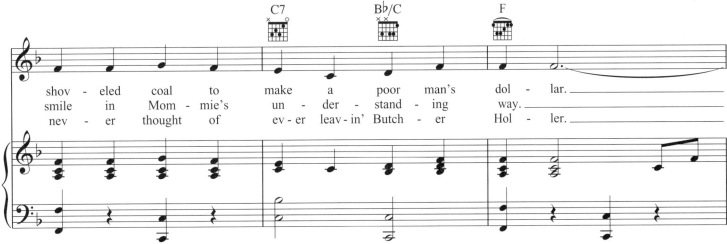

shov - eled coal to make a poor man's dol - lar. __ / smile in Mom - mie's un - der - stand - ing way. __ / nev - er thought of ev - er leav - in' Butch - er Hol - ler. __

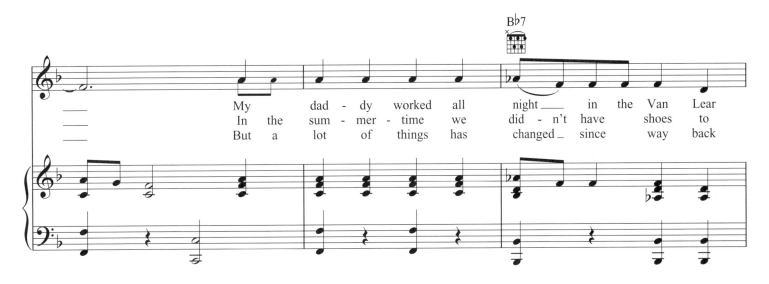

__ My dad - dy worked all night __ in the Van Lear / __ In the sum - mer - time we did - n't have shoes to / __ But a lot of things has changed __ since way back

coal mine, _____ / wear, _____ / then, _____
but in the win - ter - time we'd all / and it's so good to be
all day long in the

DRINKIN' THING

Words and Music by
WAYNE CARSON THOMPSON

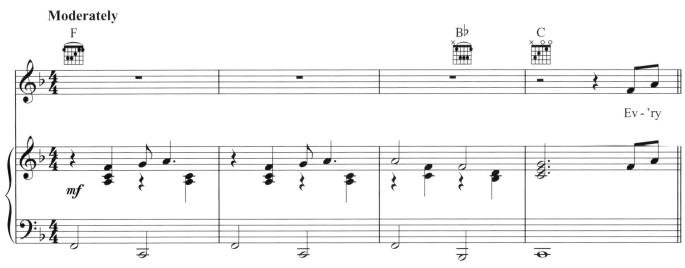

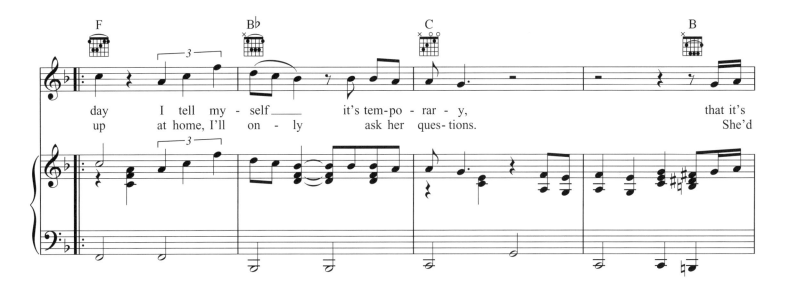

day   I tell my - self____ it's tem-po - rar - y,   that it's
up   at home, I'll on - ly   ask her ques - tions.   She'd

on - ly 'cause she's young ___   that makes her want   an - oth - er   man.
prob - 'ly tell   the   truth, ___   so I don't   e - ven   ask.

E - ven though it makes me feel __ un - nec - es - sar - y,
So I sit here on this bar - stool feel - in' help - less.

I've found a way to help me un - der - stand.}
And I won - der just how long __ a man can last.}

I've got this drink - in' thing __ to keep __ from

think - in' things __ 'bout where you've been, __ who you've

been with, and what you've done. ___ And it's a

lone - ly thing, ___ but it's ___ the on - ly thing ___

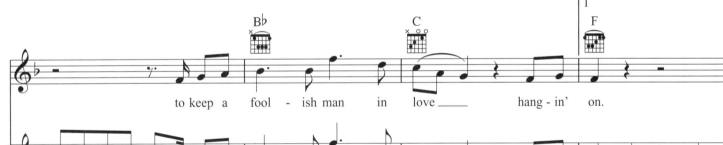

to keep a fool - ish man in love ___ hang - in' on.

If I wait on. I've got this

CONVOY

Words and Music by WILLIAM D. FRIES
and CHIP DAVIS

Moderately

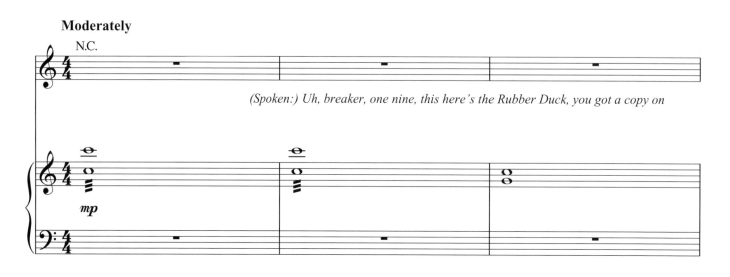

(Spoken:) Uh, breaker, one nine, this here's the Rubber Duck, you got a copy on

me, Pig-Pen, c'mon?   Uh, yeah, ten-four, Pig-Pen, fer sure, fer sure, by golly.

It's clean clear to flag town, c'mon?   Yeah,   that's a big ten-four, there, Pig-Pen, yeah,

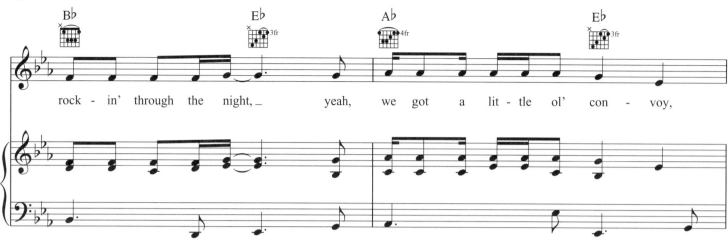

rock - in' through the night, __ yeah, we got a lit - tle ol' con - voy,

ain't she a beau - ti - ful sight? Come on and join our con - voy, ain't

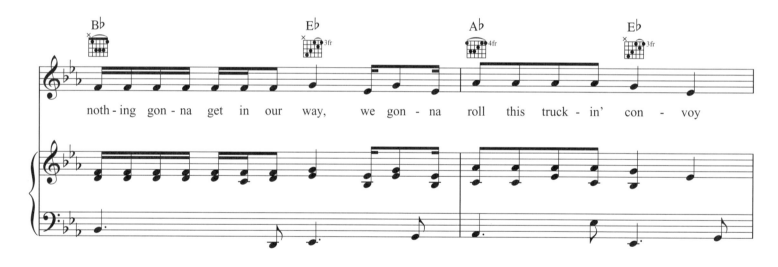

noth - ing gon - na get in our way, we gon - na roll this truck - in' con - voy

'cross the U. S. A. Con - voy, _____

(Spoken:) Breaker, Pig-Pen,   This here's the Duck an' a you wanna

20

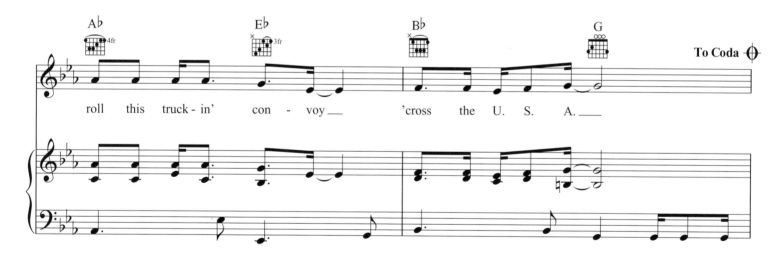

EL PASO

Words and Music by
MARTY ROBBINS

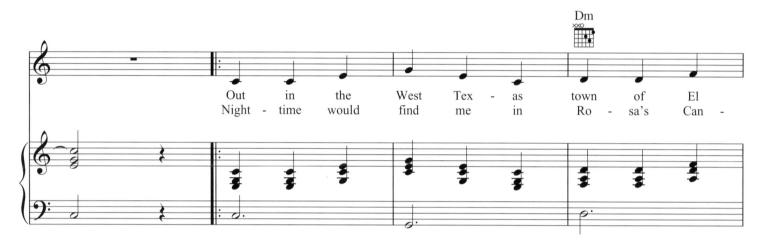

Out in the West Tex - as town of El
Night - time would find me in Ro - sa's Can -

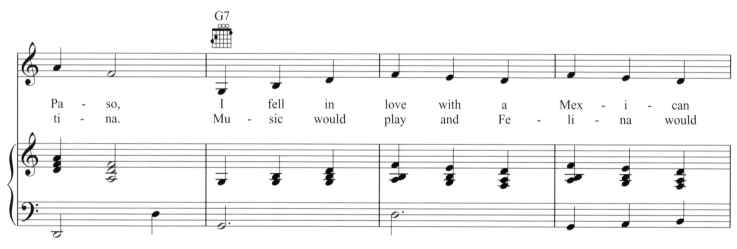

Pa - so, I fell in love with a Mex - i - can
ti - na. Mu - sic would play and Fe - li - na would

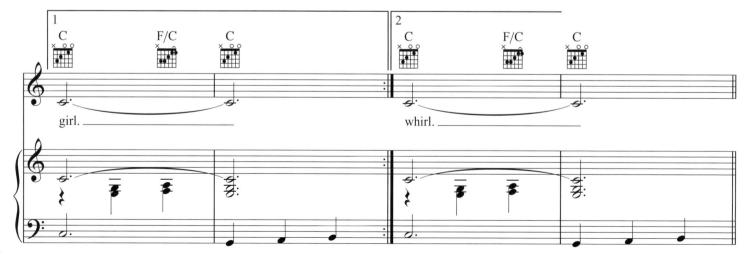

girl. _____

whirl. _____

Black - er than night were the eyes of Fe - li - na,
Just for a mo - ment, I stood there in si - lence,
Back in El Pa - so my life would be worth - less;
Off to my right I see five mount - ed cow - boys.

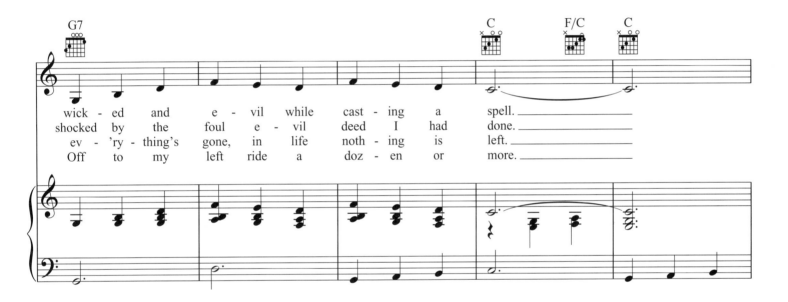

wick - ed and e - vil while cast - ing a spell. _____
shocked by the foul e - vil deed I had done. _____
ev - 'ry - thing's gone, in life noth - ing is left. _____
Off to my left ride a doz - en or more. _____

My love was deep for this Mex - i - can maid - en.
Man - y thoughts raced through my mind as I stood there.
It's been so long since I've seen the young maid - en.
Shout - ing and shoot - ing, I can't let them catch me.

I was in love, but in vain, I could tell.
I had but one chance, and that was to run.
My love is strong-er than my fear of death.
I have to make it to Ro-sa's back door.

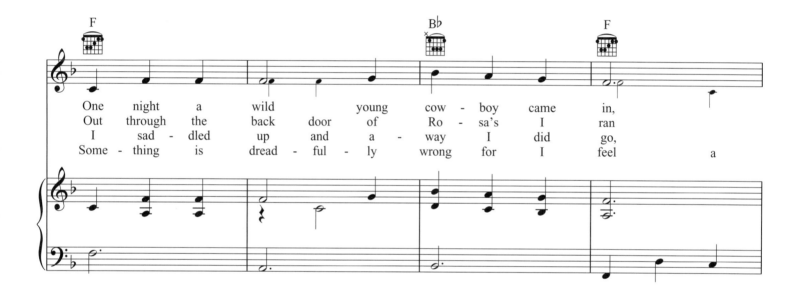

One night a wild young cow-boy came in,
Out through the wild back door of Ro-sa's I ran
I sad-dled up and a-way I did go,
Some-thing is dread-ful-ly wrong for I feel a

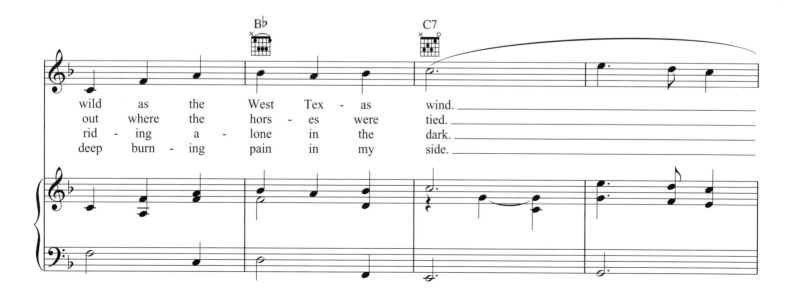

wild as the West Tex-as wind.
out where the hors-es were tied.
rid-ing a-lone in the dark.
deep burn-ing pain in my side.

Dash - ing and dar - ing, a
I caught a good one, it
May - be to - mor - row a
Though I am try - ing to

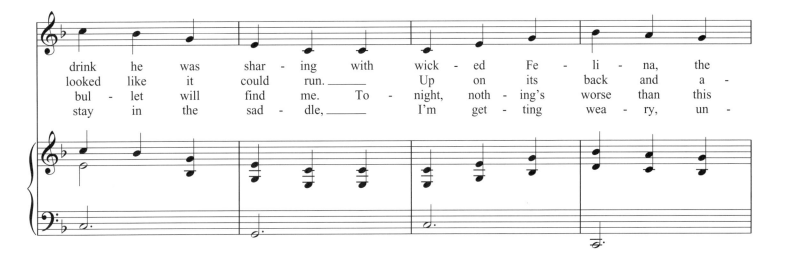

drink he was shar - ing with wick - ed Fe - li - na, the
looked like it could run. ____ Up - on its back and a -
bul - let will find me. To - night, noth - ing's worse than this
stay in the sad - dle, ____ I'm get - ting wea - ry, un -

girl that I loved. ____ So, in an - ger, I
way I did ride ____ just as fast as I
pain in my heart. ____ And at last, here I
a - ble to ride. ____ But my love for Fe -

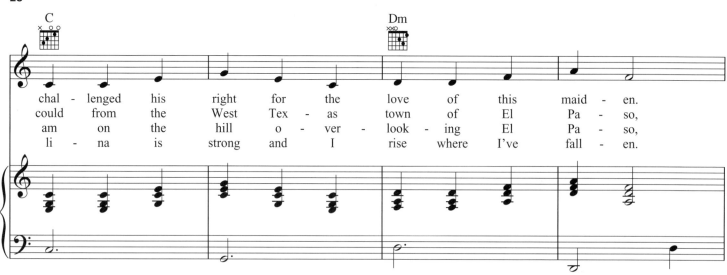

chal - lenged his right for the love of this maid - en.
could from the West Tex - as town of El Pa - so,
am on the hill o - ver - look - ing El Pa - so,
li - na is strong and I rise where I've fall - en.

Down went his hand for the gun that he wore. ____
out to the bad - lands of New Mex - i - co. ____
I can see Ro - sa's Can - ti - na be - low. ____
Though I am wea - ry, I can't stop to rest. ____

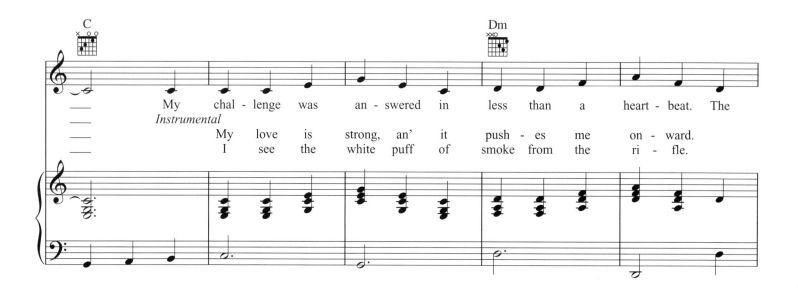

____ My chal - lenge was an - swered in less than a heart - beat. The
____ *Instrumental*
____ My love is strong, an' it push - es me on - ward.
____ I see the white puff of smoke from the ri - fle.

Play 4 times

hand - some young stran - ger lay dead on the floor. _____
Down off the hill to Fe - li - na I go. _____
I feel the bul - lct go deep in my chest. _____

Instrumental ends

From out of no - where, Fe - li - na has found me,
Cra - dled by two lov - ing arms that I'll die for,

kiss - ing my cheek as she kneels by my side. _____
one lit - tle kiss, then, Fe - li - na, good -

bye. _____

FOLSOM PRISON BLUES

Words and Music by
JOHN R. CASH

1. I hear the train a-com-in', it's roll-in' 'round the
2. I was just a ba-by, my ma-ma told me,
3.,4. (See additional lyrics)

bend, And I ain't seen the sun-shine since I don't know
"Son, _____ al-ways be a good boy; since don't ev-er play with
when.

when. I'm stuck at Fol-som Pris-on and time keeps
guns." But I shot a man in Re-no just _____ to

Additional Lyrics

3. I bet there's rich folks eatin' in a fancy dining car;
They're prob'ly drinkin' coffee and smokin' big cigars.
But I know I had it comin', I know I can't be free,
But those people keep a-movin', and that's what tortures me.

4. Well, if they freed me from this prison, if that railroad train was mine,
I bet I'd move on over a little farther down the line.
Far from Folsom Prison, that's where I want to stay,
And I'd let that lonesome whistle blow my blues away.

FRIENDS IN LOW PLACES

Words and Music by DeWAYNE BLACKWELL
and EARL BUD LEE

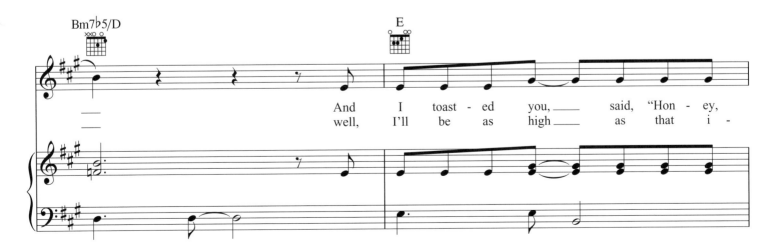

we may be through, ____ but you'll nev - er hear ____ me com - plain." ____
- vo - ry tow - er that you're liv - in' in. ____

A

____ 'Cause I've got friends ____ in low plac - es where the

whis - key ____ drowns ____ and the beer ____ chas - es my blues ____

Bm7   E

____ a - way, and I'll be o - kay. ____

Yeah, I'm not big___ on so - cial grac - es. Think I'll

slip on ___ down ___ to the o - a - sis. Oh, ___

I've got friends ___ in low ___ plac - es. ___

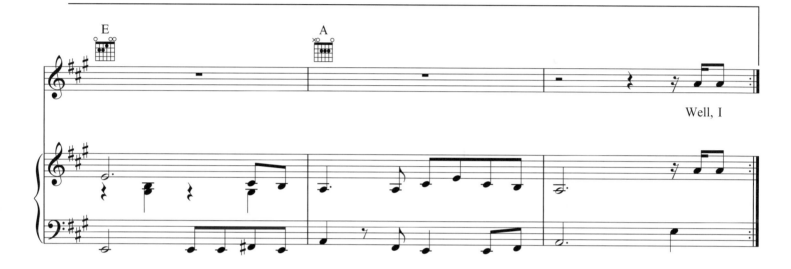

Well, I

I've got friends ___ in low plac - es where the

whis - key ___ drowns ___ and the beer ___ chas - es my blues ___

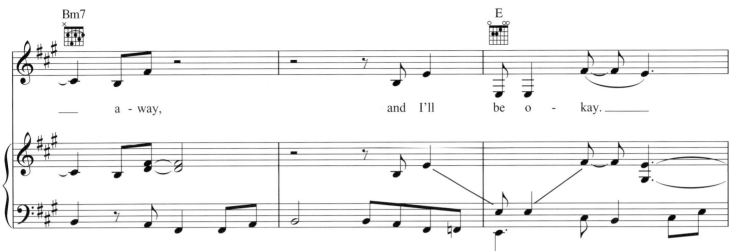

a - way, and I'll be o - kay.

Yeah, I'm not big___ on so - cial grac - es. Think I'll

slip on___ down___ to the o - a - sis. Oh,___ I've got friends___

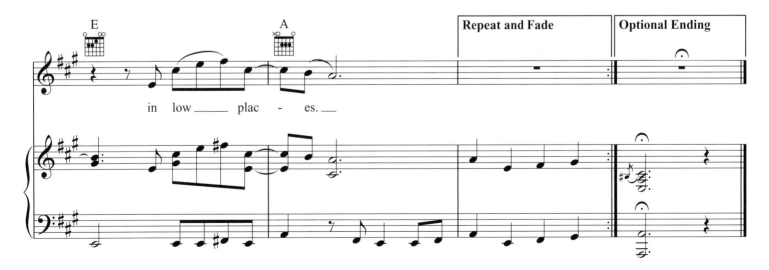

Repeat and Fade | Optional Ending

in low___ plac - es.___

A GOOD HEARTED WOMAN

Words and Music by WILLIE NELSON
and WAYLON JENNINGS

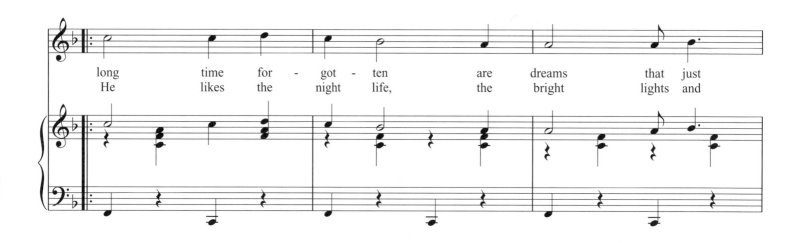

long time for -got - ten are dreams that just
He likes the night life, the bright lights and

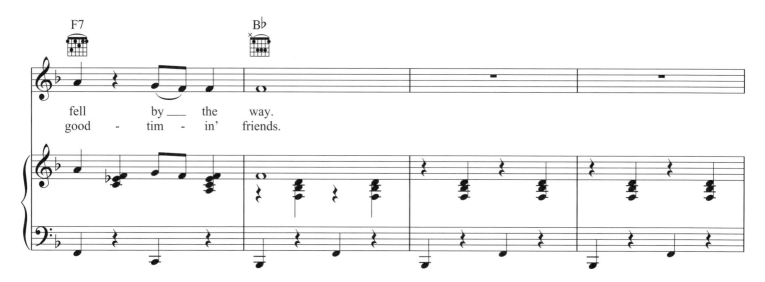

fell by ___ the way.
good - tim - in' friends.

And the good life he prom - ised
When the par - ty's all o - ver

ain't what she's liv - ing _____ to - day. _____
she'll wel - come him back home a - gain. _____

But she
Lord knows she

nev - er com - plains of the bad times or _____
don't un - der - stand him, but she does the _____

bad things ___ he's done, Lord.
best that ___ she can. ___

She just talks a - bout the
'Cause she's a good - heart - ed

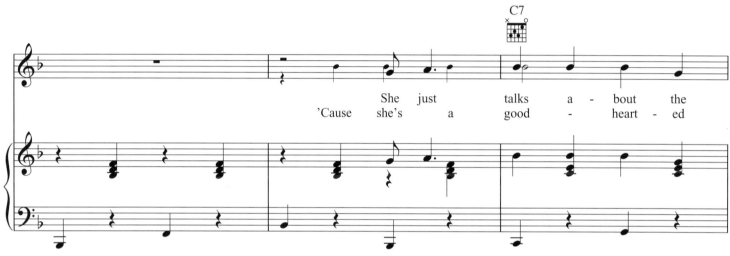

good times they've had and all the good times to ___
wom - an; she loves her good - tim - in' ___

come.
man. She's a

good - heart - ed wom - an __ in love with a good - tim - in'

man. She

loves him in spite of his ways that she don't un - der -

stand. Through

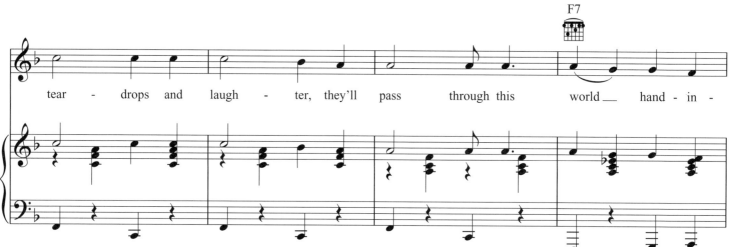

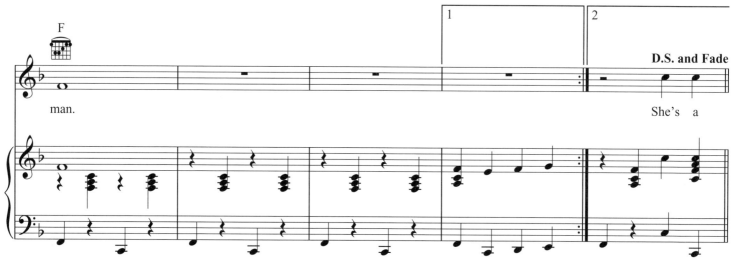

GUITARS, CADILLACS

Words and Music by
DWIGHT YOAKAM

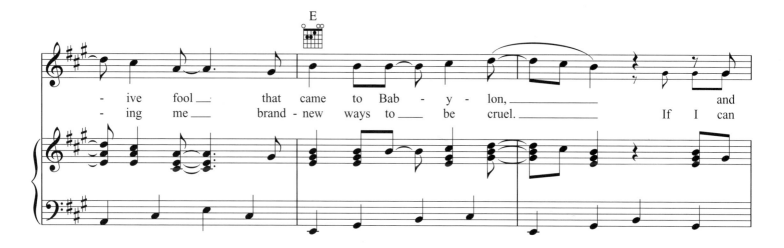

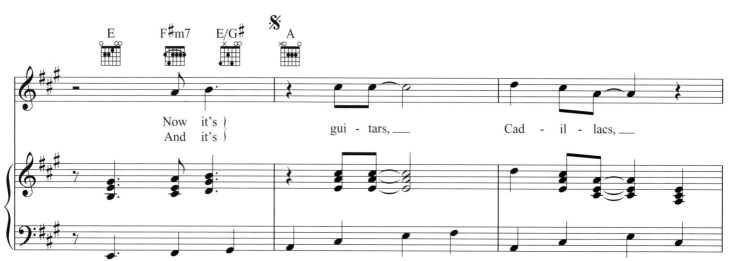

hill - bil - ly mu - sic ___ and lone - ly, lone - ly streets ___

___ that I ___ call home. ___ Yeah, my

gui - tars, ___ Cad - il - lacs, ___ hill - bil - ly

To Coda ⊕

mu - sic ___ is the on - ly thing ___ that keeps ___ me hang - in' on. ___

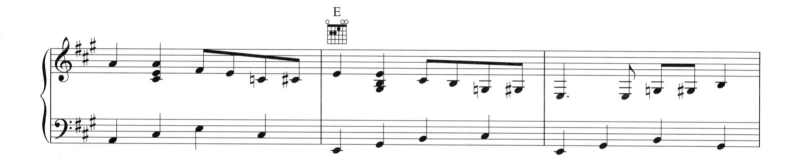

There ain't no glam -

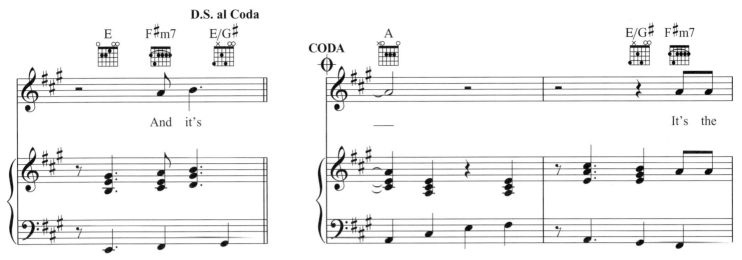

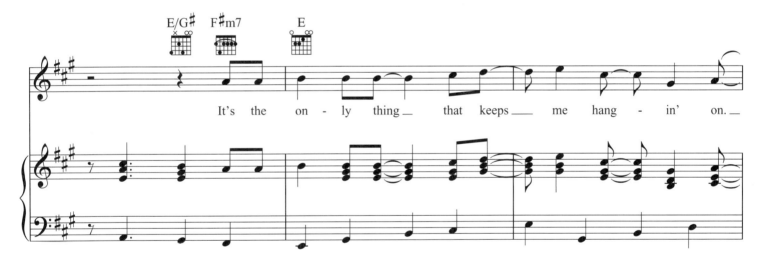

HEY, GOOD LOOKIN'

Words and Music by
HANK WILLIAMS

Hey, hey, good look-in',
free and read-y so

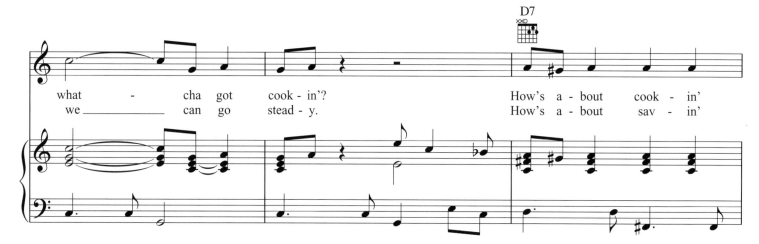

what - cha got cook-in'?
we _____ can go stead-y.
How's a-bout cook-in'
How's a-bout sav-in'

some - thin' up ____ with me? ____
all your time ____ for me? ____

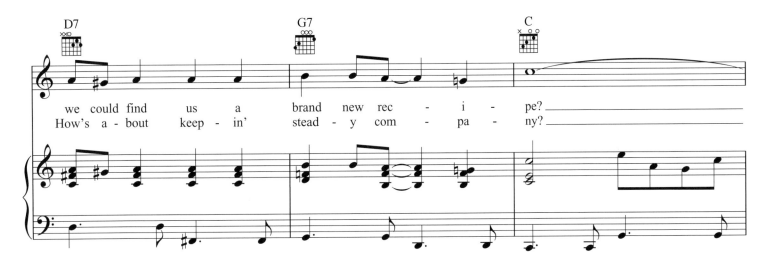

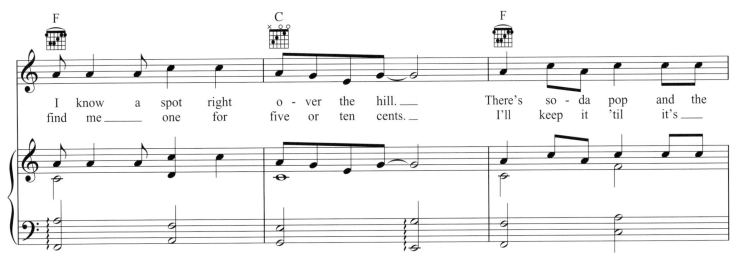

danc - in's free, so if you wan - na have fun come a - long with me. —

cov - ered with age _____ 'cause I'm writ - in' your name down on ev - 'ry page. —

Hey, good look - in', what - cha got cook - in'?

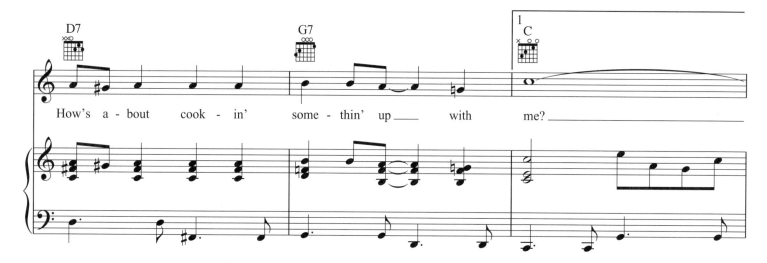

How's a - bout cook - in' some - thin' up _____ with me? _____

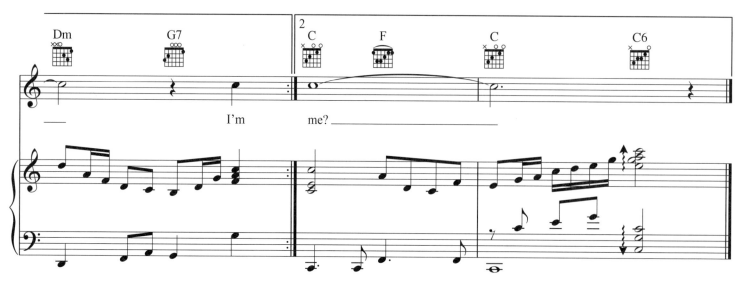

_____ I'm me? _____

JOLENE

Words and Music by
DOLLY PARTON

Jo - lene, Jo - lene, Jo - lene, Jo -

lene, _____ I'm beg-ging of you, please don't take my man. _____

Jo - lene, Jo - lene, Jo - lene, Jo -

lene, _____ please don't take him just be-cause you can. _____

Your beau - ty is be - yond com - pare, with
You could have your choice of men, but

flam - ing locks of au - burn hair, with i - v'ry skin and eyes of em - 'rald
I could nev - er love a - gain. ____ He's the on - ly one for me, Jo -

green. _____
lene. _____

Your smile is like a breath of spring, your
I had to have this talk with you, my

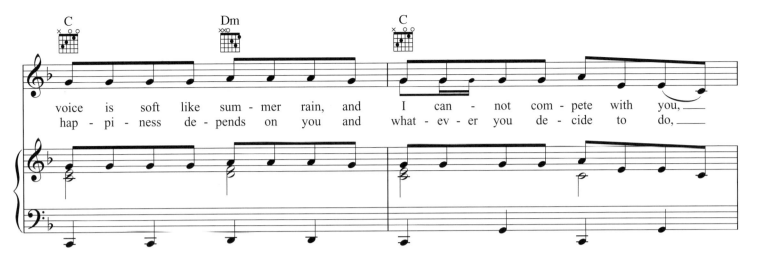

voice is soft like sum - mer rain, and I can - not com - pete with you,___
hap - pi - ness de - pends on you and what - ev - er you de - cide to do,___

To Coda

Jo - lene.
Jo - lene.

He
Jo -

talks a - bout you in his sleep and there's noth - ing I can do to keep from

cry - in' when he calls your name, Jo - lene.___

And

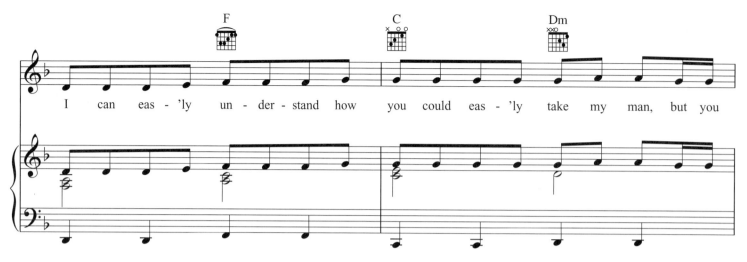

I can eas - 'ly un - der - stand how you could eas - 'ly take my man, but you

D.S. al Coda

don't know what he means to me, Jo - lene. Jo -

CODA

lene, Jo - lene, Jo - lene, Jo - lene, _____ I'm

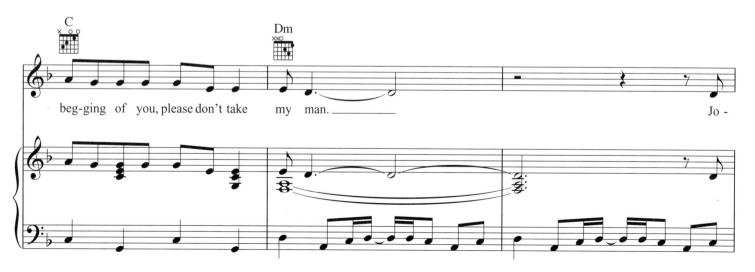

beg - ging of you, please don't take my man. _____ Jo -

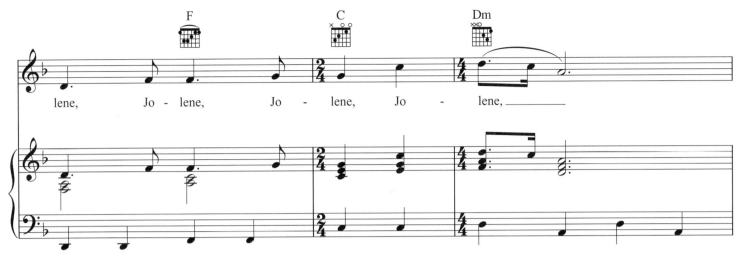

lene,   Jo - lene,   Jo - lene,   Jo - lene, _____

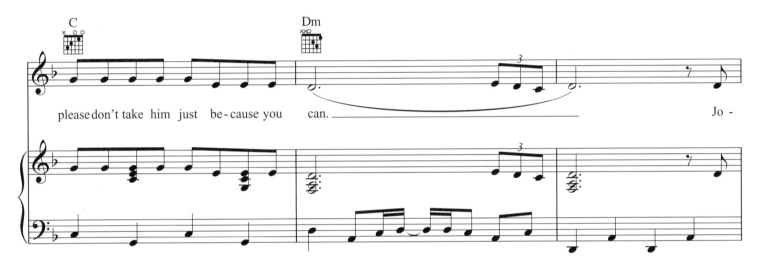

please don't take him just be - cause you   can. _____   Jo -

lene,   Jo - lene,   please don't take my man, Jo - lene,   Jo -

lene,   Jo - lene.   My hap - pi - ness de - pends on you, Jo - lene.

HONKY TONK HEROES

Words and Music by
BILLY JOE SHAVER

Moderately

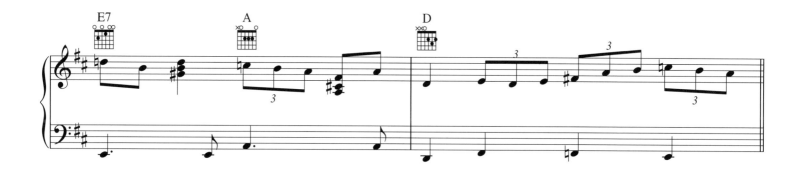

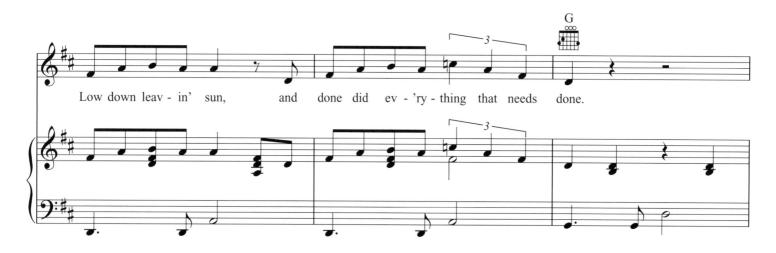

Low down leav- in' sun, and done did ev- 'ry- thing that needs done.

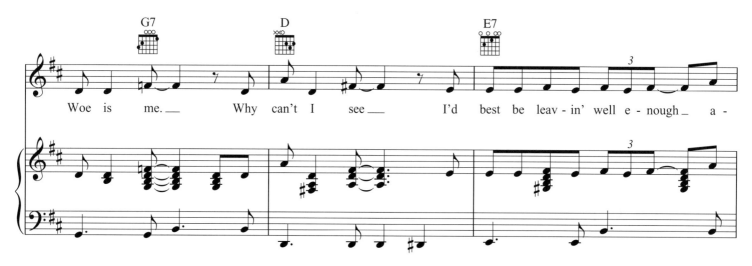

Woe is me. ___ Why can't I see ___ I'd best be leav- in' well e- nough ___ a-

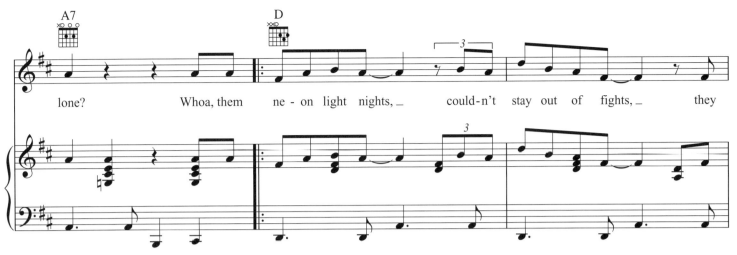

lone? Whoa, them ne - on light nights, __ could-n't stay out of fights, __ they

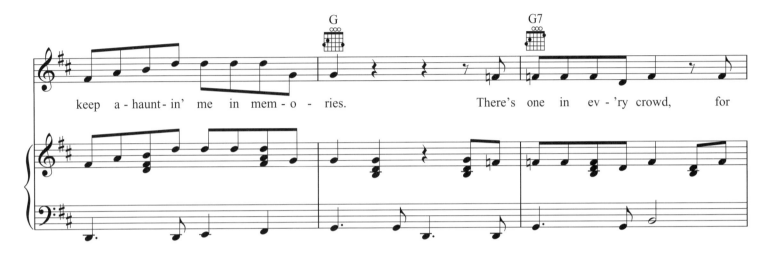

keep a - haunt-in' me in mem - o - ries. There's one in ev - 'ry crowd, for

cry - in' out loud. __ Why was it al - ways turn-in' out to be me? __ Oh,

where does it go? ___ The good Lord ___ on - ly knows. It

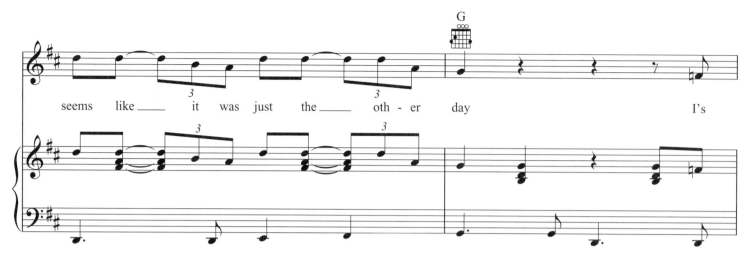

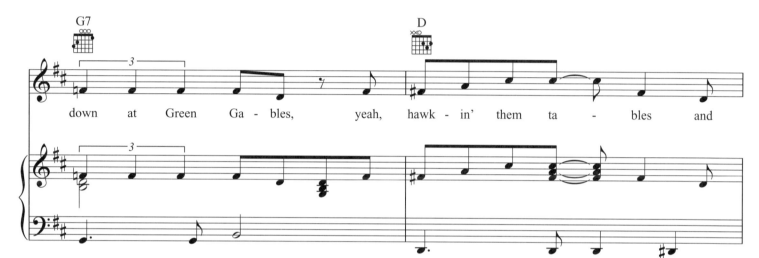

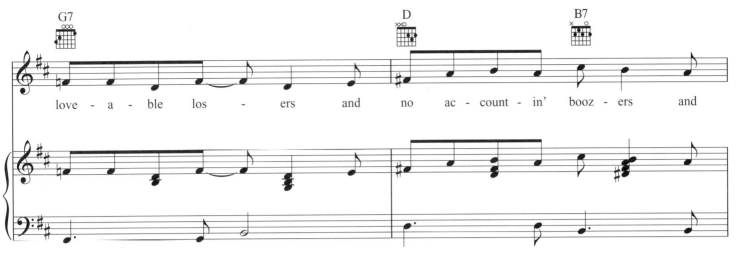

love - a - ble los - ers and no ac - count - in' booz - ers and

hon - ky - tonk he - roes like me. Whoa, them

me.

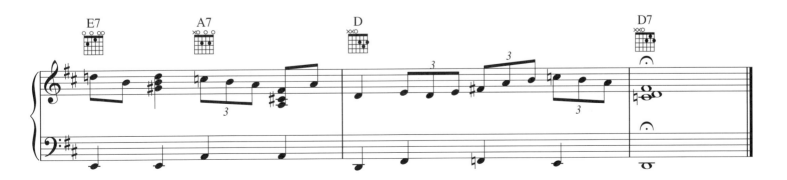

I THINK I'LL JUST STAY HERE AND DRINK

Words and Music by
MERLE HAGGARD

Could be hold-ing you to - night.
hear

Could quit do-ing wrong, start do-ing right. _____ You don't care a-bout what I
that loud juke box play - in' in my ear. _____ Ain't no wom-an gon' change the

think.
way I think.

Think I'll just _ stay here and _ drink.
Think I'll just _ stay here and _ drink.

KING OF THE ROAD

Words and Music by
ROGER MILLER

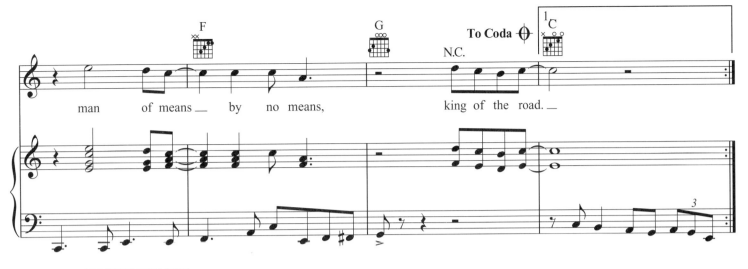

man of means __ by no means, king of the road. __

__ I know ev - er - y en - gi - neer on ev - er - y train, __ all of the chil - dren and

all of their names, __ and ev - er - y hand - out in ev - er - y town, __ and

ev - 'ry lock that ain't locked when no one's a - round. __ I sing:

LONG HAIRED COUNTRY BOY

Words and Music by
CHARLIE DANIELS

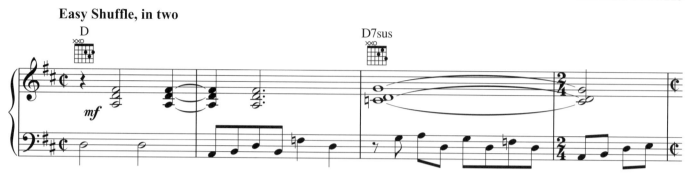

Peo-ple say I'm no good, I'm cra-zy as a loon, 'cause

I get stoned in the morn-ing, I get drunk in the af-ter-noon.

Kind-a like ___ my old blue tick hound, ___ I like to lay a - round in the shade. ___ And

I ain't got no ___ mon - ey, ___ but I damn sure got it ___ made. ___ 'Cause I ain't ask -

- in' no - bod - y for noth - in' if I can't ___ get it on my

own. ___ If you don't ___

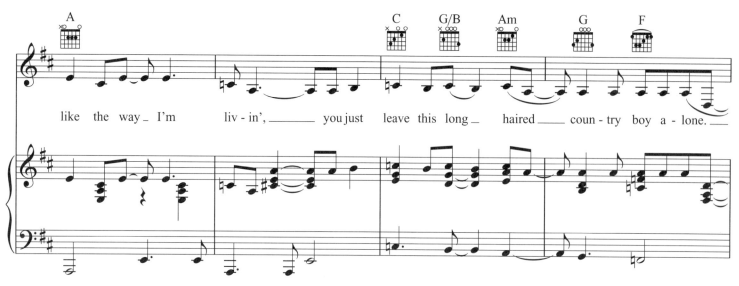

like the way _ I'm liv-in', _____ you just leave this long _ haired _____ coun-try boy a-lone. __

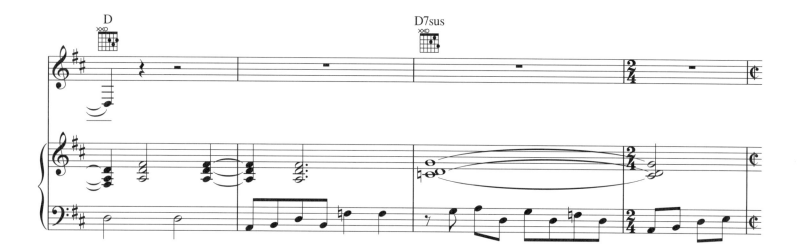

Preach-er man talk-ing on T. V., puttin' down the rock and roll. __

own. _____ If you don't _____

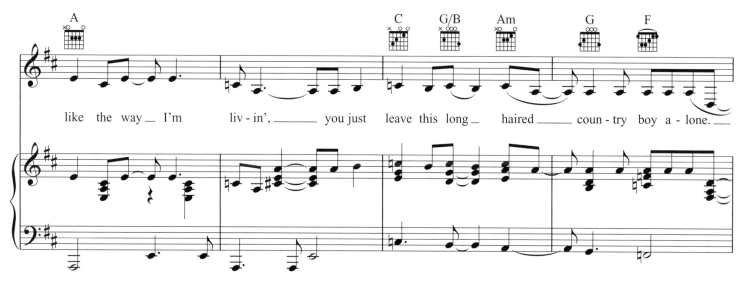

like the way _____ I'm liv-in', _____ you just leave this long _____ haired _____ coun-try boy a-lone. _____

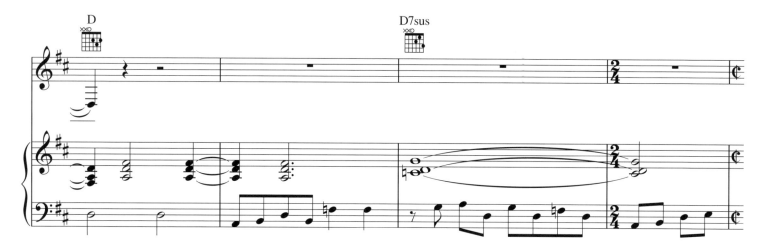

poor girl wants to mar - ry____ and a rich girl___ wants to flirt.___ A

rich man goes to col - lege____ and a poor man goes to work. A

drunk-ard wants_ an-oth-er drink of wine_ and a pol-i-ti-cian wants your vote.___

I don't want_ much of noth-ing at all,_ but I will take an-oth - er toke.___ But I ain't ask-

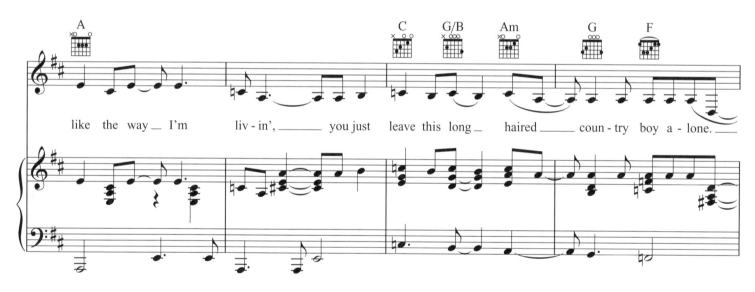

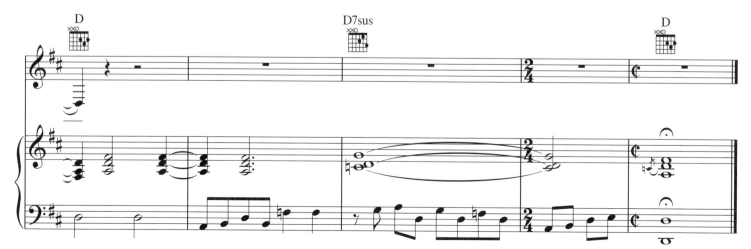

STREETS OF BAKERSFIELD

Words and Music by
HOMER JOY

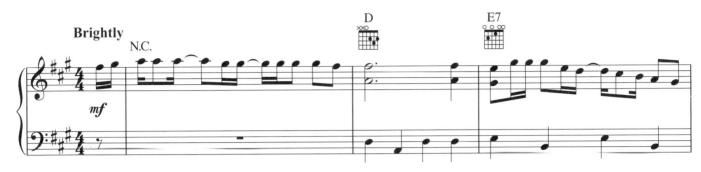

I came here look-ing for some-thing _____
Spent some time in San Fran-cis- co, _____

I could-n't find an-y-where else. _____ Hey, I'm not try'ng to be no-
spent a night there in the can. _____ They threw this drunk man in my

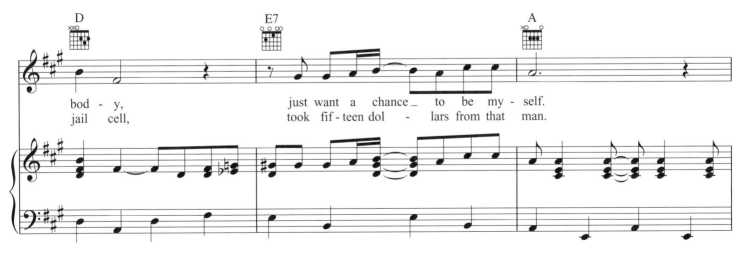

bod - y, just want a chance _ to be my - self.
jail cell, took fif-teen dol - lars from that man.

I've done a thou-sand miles of thumb-in',
Left him my watch and my old house key,

I've worn holes in both my
don't want folks think-in' that I'd

heels,
steal.

Try'ng to find me some-thing bet-ter _____
Then I thanked him as I was leav-ing, _____

on the streets of Ba-kers-field.
and I head-ed for the streets of Ba-kers-field.

Oh, you don't know me but you don't like me.

You say you care less how I

feel. _____

But how man-y of you that sit and judge me

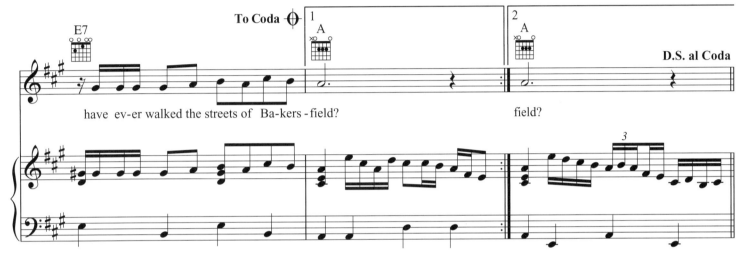

To Coda ⊕

1.

have ev-er walked the streets of Ba-kers-field?

2.

D.S. al Coda

field?

CODA ⊕

field?

How man-y of you that sit and judge me

have ev-er walked the streets of Ba-kers - field?

LOUISIANA WOMAN, MISSISSIPPI MAN

Words and Music by JIM OWEN
and BECKI BLUEFIELD

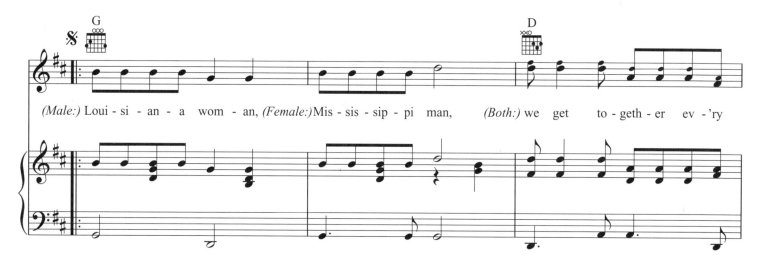

(Male:) Loui-si-an-a wom-an, (Female:) Mis-sis-sip-pi man, (Both:) we get to-geth-er ev-'ry

time we can. ___ The Mis-sis-sip-pi Riv-er can't keep us a-part, ___ (Male:) there's

* *Recorded a half step lower.*

MAKE THE WORLD GO AWAY

Words and Music by
HANK COCHRAN

MAMA TRIED

Words and Music by
MERLE HAGGARD

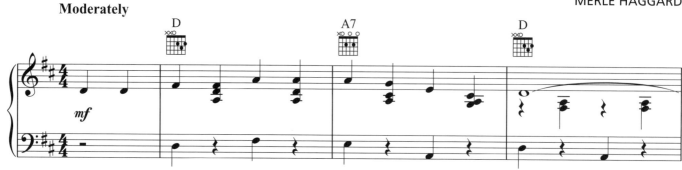

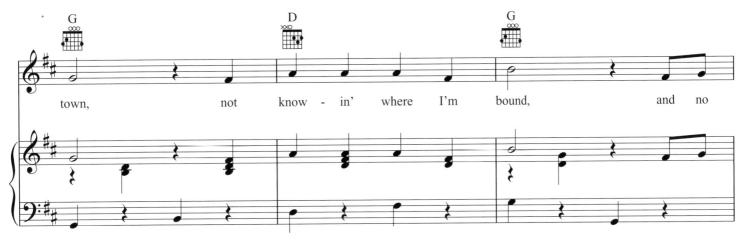

town,   not know - in' where I'm bound,   and no

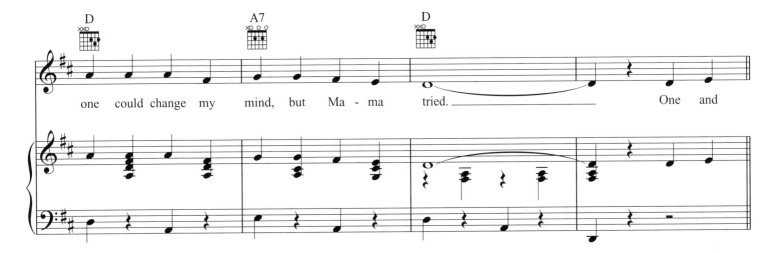

one could change my mind, but Ma - ma tried. _____ One and

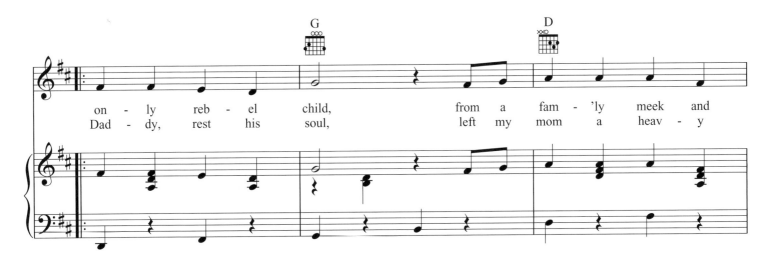

on - ly reb - el child,   from a fam - 'ly meek and
Dad - dy, rest his soul,   left my mom a heav - y

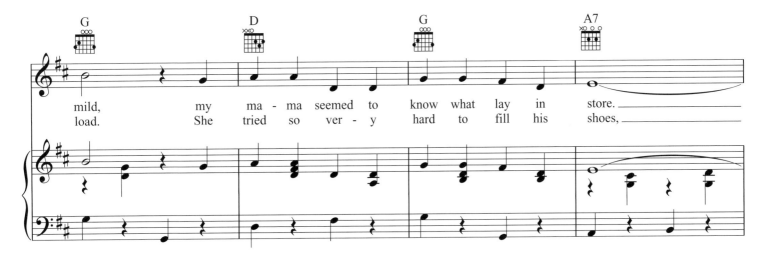

mild,   my ma - ma seemed to know what lay in store. _____
load.   She tried so ver - y hard to fill his shoes, _____

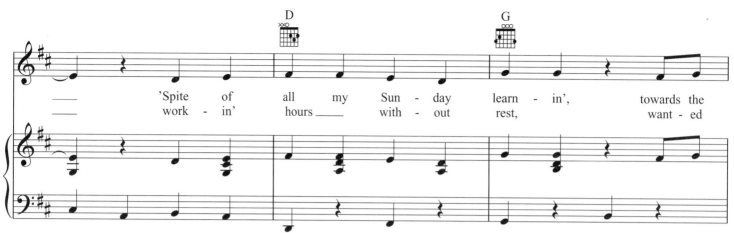

'Spite of all my Sun - day learn - in', towards the
work - in' hours _____ with - out rest, want - ed

bad I kept on turn - in', 'til Ma - ma could - n't hold me an - y -
me to have the best. She tried to raise me right, but I re -

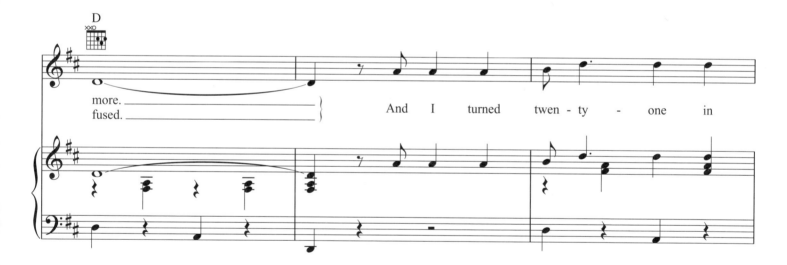

more. _____ And I turned twen - ty - one in
fused. _____

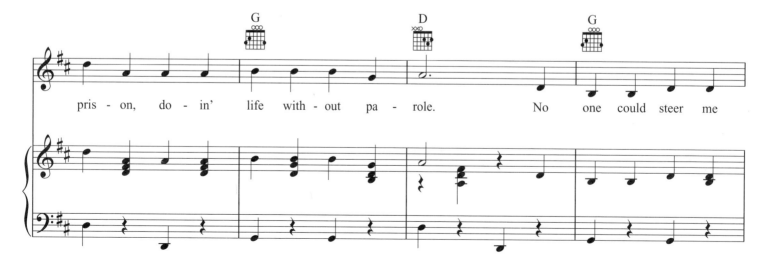

pris - on, do - in' life with - out pa - role. No one could steer me

ME AND PAUL

Words and Music by
WILLIE NELSON

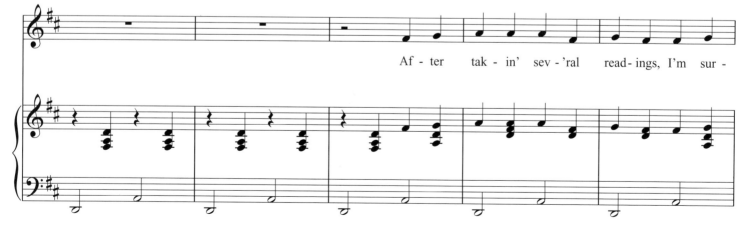

prised to find my mind still fair - ly sound.

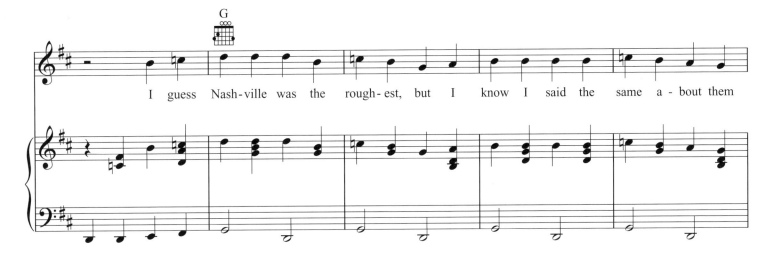

I guess Nash - ville was the rough - est, but I know I said the same a - bout them

all. We re - ceived our ed - u - ca - tion in the

cit - ies of the na - tion, me and Paul.

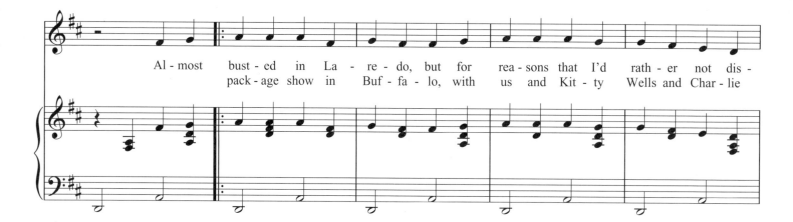

Al - most bust - ed in La - re - do, but for rea - sons that I'd rath - er not dis -
pack - age show in Buf - fa - lo, with us and Kit - ty Wells and Char - lie

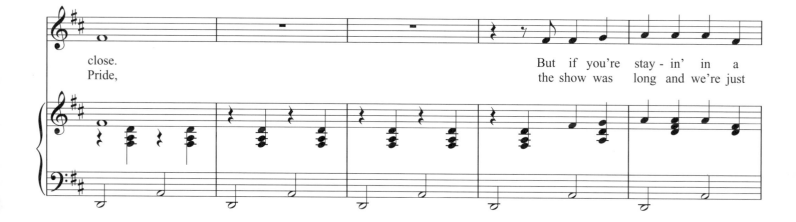

close.
Pride,

But if you're stay - in' in a
the show was long and we're just

D7

mo - tel there and leave, just don't leave noth - in' in your clothes.
sit - tin' there and we'd come to play and not just for the ride.

G

And at the air - port in Mil -
Well, we'd drank a lot _____ of

MY HEROES HAVE ALWAYS BEEN COWBOYS

Words and Music by
SHARON VAUGHN

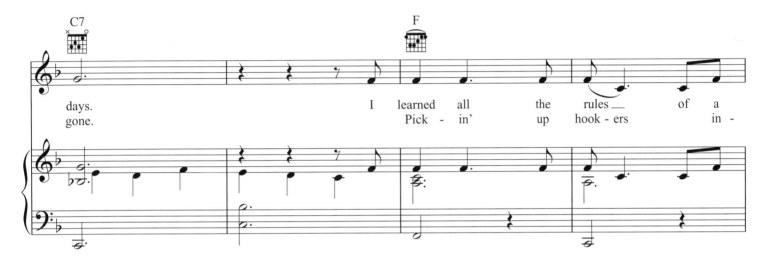

la - dies then leave them with the words   of a sad coun - try
old worn - out mem - 'ries _____ with no one   and no place to

song. }
stay. }
My he - roes _____ have al - ways been

cow - boys, _____   and they still are, it

seems.   Sad - ly _____ in search of _____ and

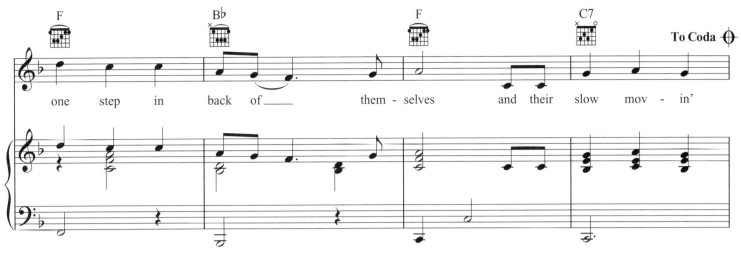

one step in back of _____ them - selves and their slow mov - in'

dreams.

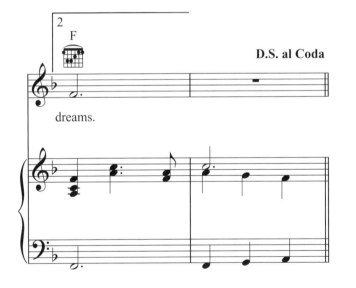

dreams.

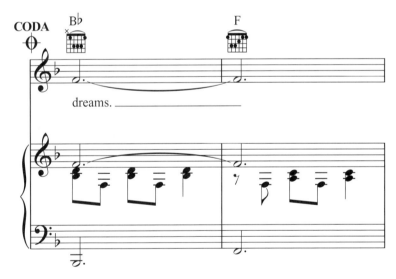

dreams. _____

NINE TO FIVE

Words and Music by
DOLLY PARTON

out on the street, the traf - fic starts jump-ing, with folks ___ like me on the
wait - in' for the day your ___ ship -'ll come in, and the tide's gon - na turn and

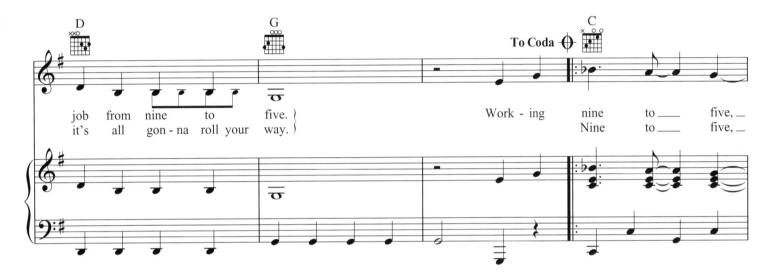

job from nine to five. }
it's all gon - na roll your way. }

Work - ing nine to ___ five, ___
Nine to ___ five, ___

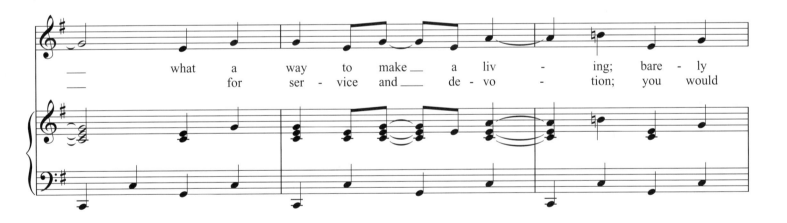

___ what a way to make ___ a liv - ing; bare - ly
___ for ser - vice and ___ de - vo - tion; you would

get - ting by, ___ it's all tak - ing and ___ no giv - ing. They just
think ___ that I ___ would de - serve a fair ___ pro - mo - tion. Want to

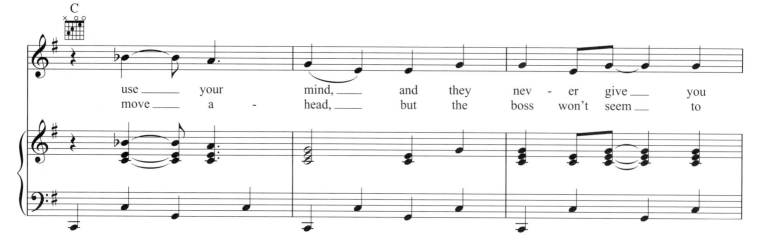

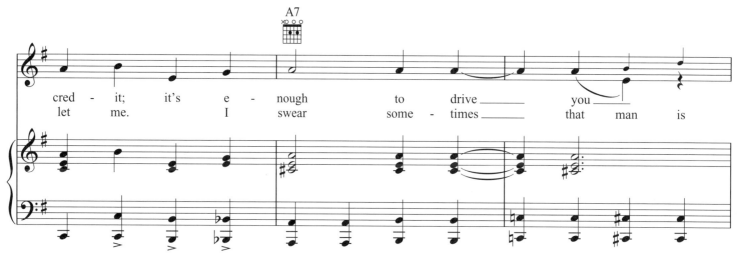

ON THE ROAD AGAIN

Words and Music by
WILLIE NELSON

love is mak - ing mu - sic with my friends, and I can't wait to get

things that I may nev - er see a - gain, and I can't wait to get

on the road ___ a - gain. ___ On the

on the road ___ a - gain. ___ gain. ___

Solo ends

On the road a - gain. ___ Like a band of gyp - sies,

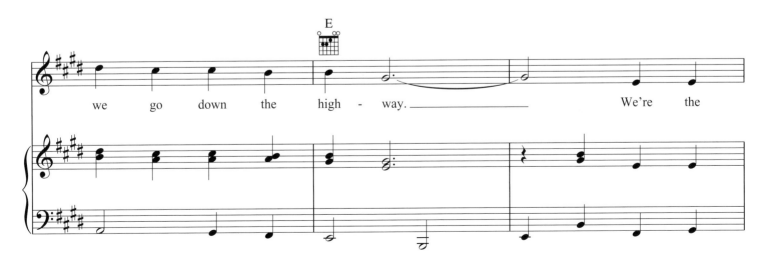

we go down the high - way. ___ We're the

98

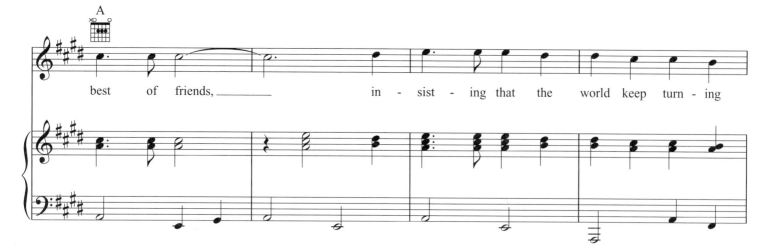

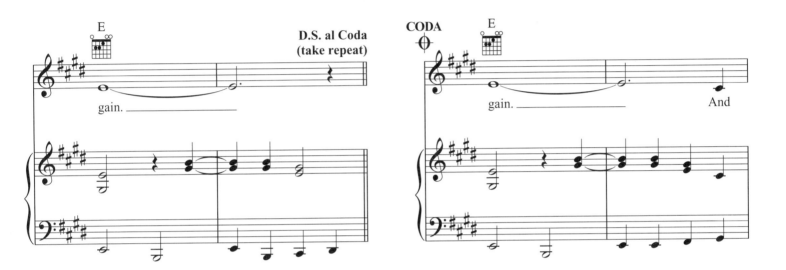

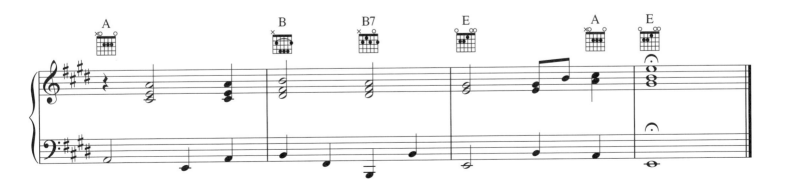

REDNECKS, WHITE SOCKS AND BLUE RIBBON BEER

Words and Music by CHUCK NEESE,
BOB McDILL and WAYLAND HOLYFIELD

Lively, with humor

and the cig - a - rette _ smoke kind - a hangs _____ in __ the air. __

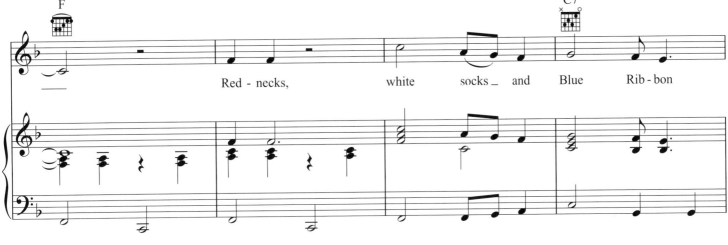

Red - necks, white socks _ and Blue Rib - bon

beer. A cow - boy is cuss - in' __ the
sem - is _ are pass - ing _ on the

pin - ball ma - chine. __
high - way out - side. __ The four - thir - ty crowd _ is a -
A drunk at the bar __ is get - tin'

noi - sy and __ mean, and some guy on the phone __
bout to __ ar - rive. __ The sun's go - in' down __

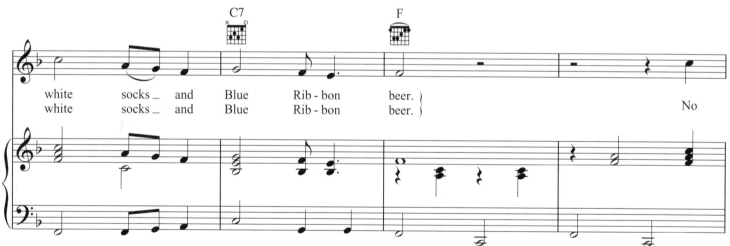

_____ says, "I'll _____ be __ home __ soon __ dear." Red - necks,
_____ and we'll soon __ all __ be __ here. Red - necks,

white socks __ and Blue Rib - bon beer.
white socks __ and Blue Rib - bon beer. No

we don't fit in _____ with that white col - lar crowd. _____ We're a

lit - tle ___ too row - dy and a lit - tle too ___

loud, but there's no place that I'd ___ rath-er be ___ than right ___

here with my red - neck, white socks ___ and Blue Rib - bon

1
beer.   The beer.

2
beer. ___

SIX DAYS ON THE ROAD

Words and Music by EARL GREEN
and CARL MONTGOMERY

speed zone a-head, but al-right. ___ I don't see a cop in sight. ___

passed a ___ "Jim-my" and a "White." I been pass-in' ev-'ry-thing in sight. ___ Six

1 - 4

days on the road and I'm a-gon-na make it home to-night. ___ 2. I got me

5

Additional Lyrics

3. Well, it seems like a month since I kissed my baby goodbye.
I could have a lot of women, but I'm not alike some other guys.
I could find me one to hold me tight,
But I could never make believe it's alright,
Six days on the road and I'm a-gonna make it home tonight.

4. Well, the I.C.C. is checking on down the line.
I'm a little overweight and my log book's way behind.
But nothing bothers me tonight,
I can dodge all the scales alright.
Six days on the road and I'm a-gonna make it home tonight.

5. Well, my rig's a little old, but that don't mean she's slow.
There's a flame from her stack, and that smoke's blowin' black as coal.
My home town's coming in sight:
If you think I'm happy, you're right.
Six days on the road and I'm a-gonna make it home tonight.

T FOR TEXAS

Words and Music by
JIMMIE RODGERS

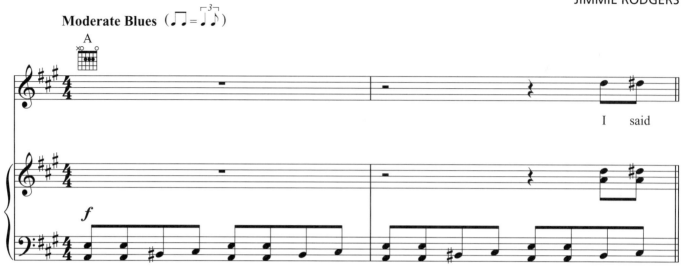

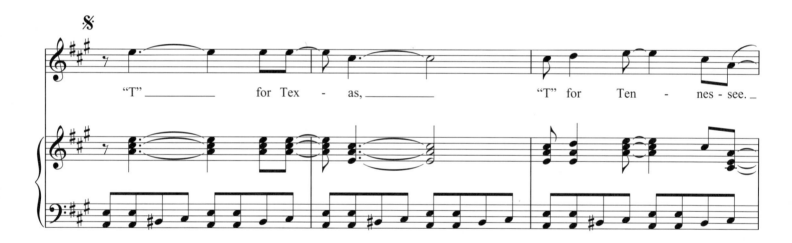

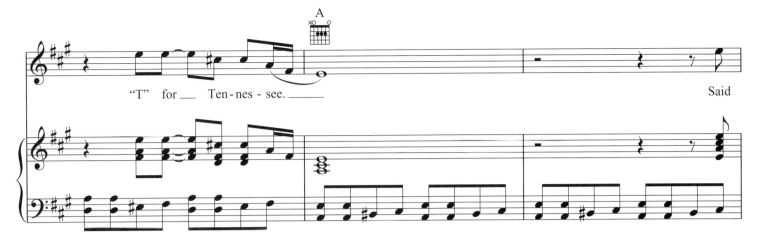

"T" for __ Ten-nes-see. _____   Said

"T" _____ for __ Thel-ma,   the gal who made a wreck __ out of me. _

___   1. Well, if __ you don't __ want __ me, ma -
                                                 2.-4. *(See additional lyrics)*

- ma,   you sure don't   have _____ to start.

Oh, you don't want me, ma - ma, you

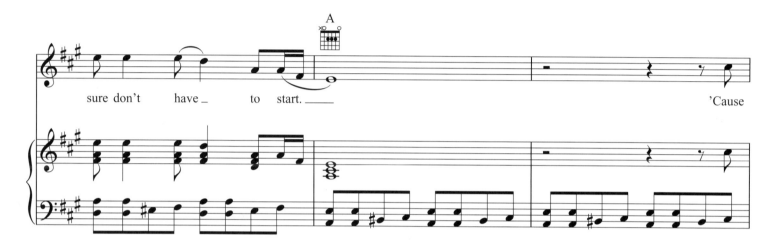

sure don't have _ to start. _____ 'Cause

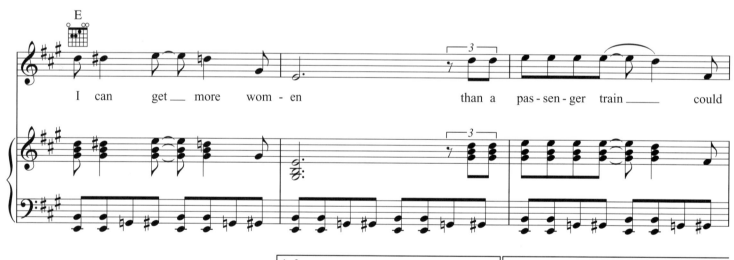

I can get _ more wom - en than a pas - sen - ger train _____ could

haul.

I'm gon - na
I'm gon - na
I'm go - ing

I said

Oh yeah, __ wom-en make __ a

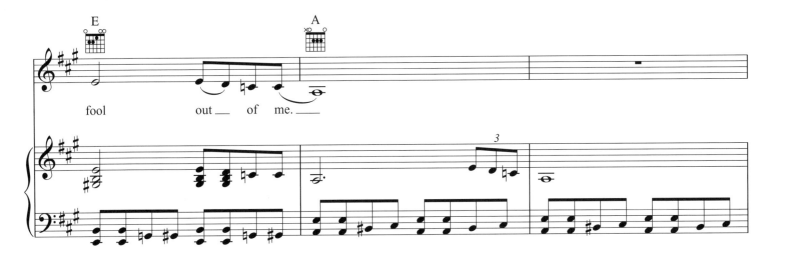

fool out __ of me. __

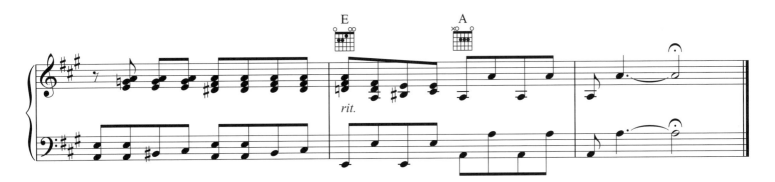

rit.

Additional Lyrics

2. I'm gonna buy me a pistol,
   Just as long as I am tall.
   I'm gonna buy me a pistol,
   Just as long as I am tall.
   I'm gonna shoot down old, mean Thelma
   Just to watch her jump and fall.

3. I'm gonna buy me a shotgun
   With a great, long, shiny barrel.
   I'm gonna buy me a shotgun
   With a great, long, shiny barrel.
   Gonna shoot down that rounder
   That stole my girl.

4. I'm going where the water
   Tastes like cherry wine.
   I'm going where the water
   Tastes like cherry wine.
   'Cause the water down here in Georgia
   Tastes like turpentine.

TWO MORE BOTTLES OF WINE

Words and Music by
DELBERT McCLINTON

Moderate Country Rock

We came out ___ west to-geth - er with a com-mon de-sire. ___
way he left sure ___ turned ___ my ___ head a - round. ___

The fe - ver we had ___ might-a
Seemed like o - ver-night he just

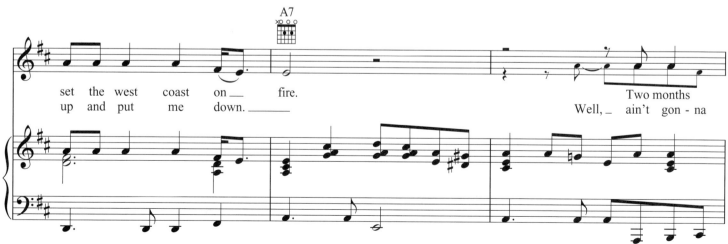

set the west coast on ___ fire.
up and put me down. ___

Two months
Well, ___ ain't gon - na

from the peo - ple I know. I've been

do - in' all I can, but op - por - tu - ni - ty sure comes slow.

Thought I'd be in the sun all day, but I'm

sweep-in' out a ware-house in West L. A. But it's al - right, 'cause it's

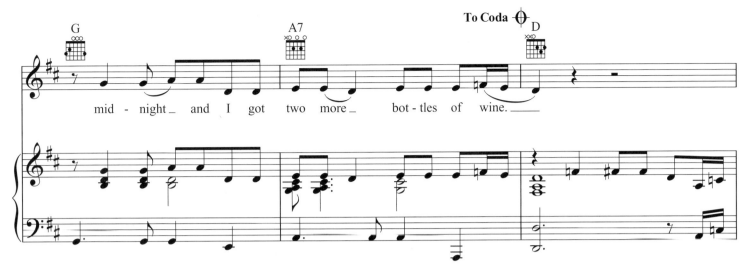

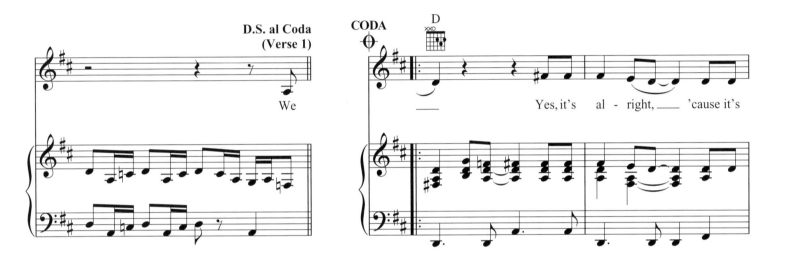

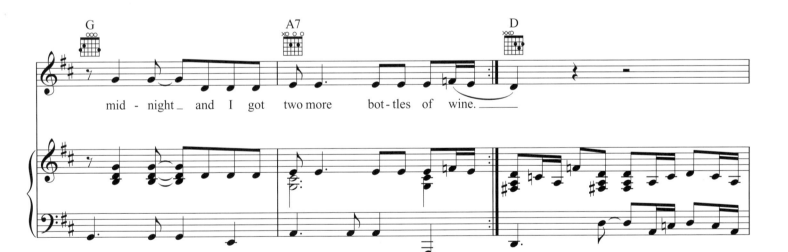

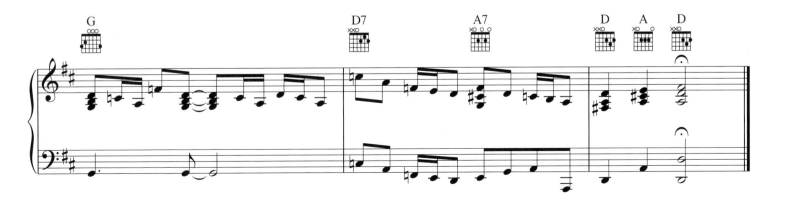

TAKE THIS JOB AND SHOVE IT

Words and Music by
DAVID ALLEN COE

WHITE LIGHTNING

Words and Music by
J.P. RICHARDSON

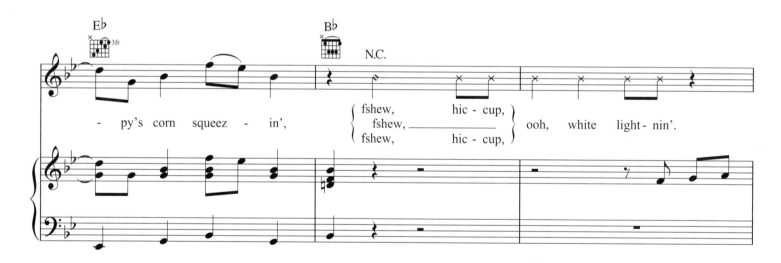